TOON INTO READING!™

# SOMETHING'S FISHY

Giggle and LEARN

A TOON BOOK BY KEVIN McCLOSKEY

Also look for: *THE REAL POOP ON PIGEONS!*, *WE DIG WORMS!*, *SNAILS ARE JUST MY SPEED,* and *ANTS DON'T WEAR PANTS!*, which together with *SOMETHING'S FISHY* are the bestselling **GIGGLE AND LEARN** series by Kevin McCloskey

FOR MRS. BERNETTA O'BRIEN, MY KINDERGARTEN TEACHER, WHO LET ME DRAW ON THE CHALKBOARD.

Editorial Director & Designer: FRANÇOISE MOULY
Title Lettering: ALA LEE
KEVIN McCLOSKEY's artwork was painted with acrylics and gouache on Fabriano art paper.

A TOON BOOK

Library of Congress Cataloging-in-Publication Data: McCloskey, Kevin, author. Something's fishy : a TOON book / by Kevin McCloskey. New York, NY : TOON Books, 2017. | Summary: In another offering of the *Giggle and Learn* series, Kevin McCloskey blends science, art, and comedy to reveal the true story behind the common goldfish.–Provided by publisher. Series: Giggle and learn Identifiers: LCCN 2016037010 | ISBN 9781943145157 (hardcover : alk. paper) Subjects: LCSH: Fishes--Juvenile literature. | Goldfish--Juvenile literature. Classification: LCC QL617.2 .M363 2017 | DDC 597--dc23 LC record available at https://lccn.loc.gov/2016037010. Printed in China. First paperback edition, 2023.

ISBN 978-1-943145-15-7 (hardcover)
ISBN 978-1-6626-6512-7 (paperback)
10 9 8 7 6 5 4 3 2 1
www.TOON-BOOKS.com

# SOMETHING'S FISHY

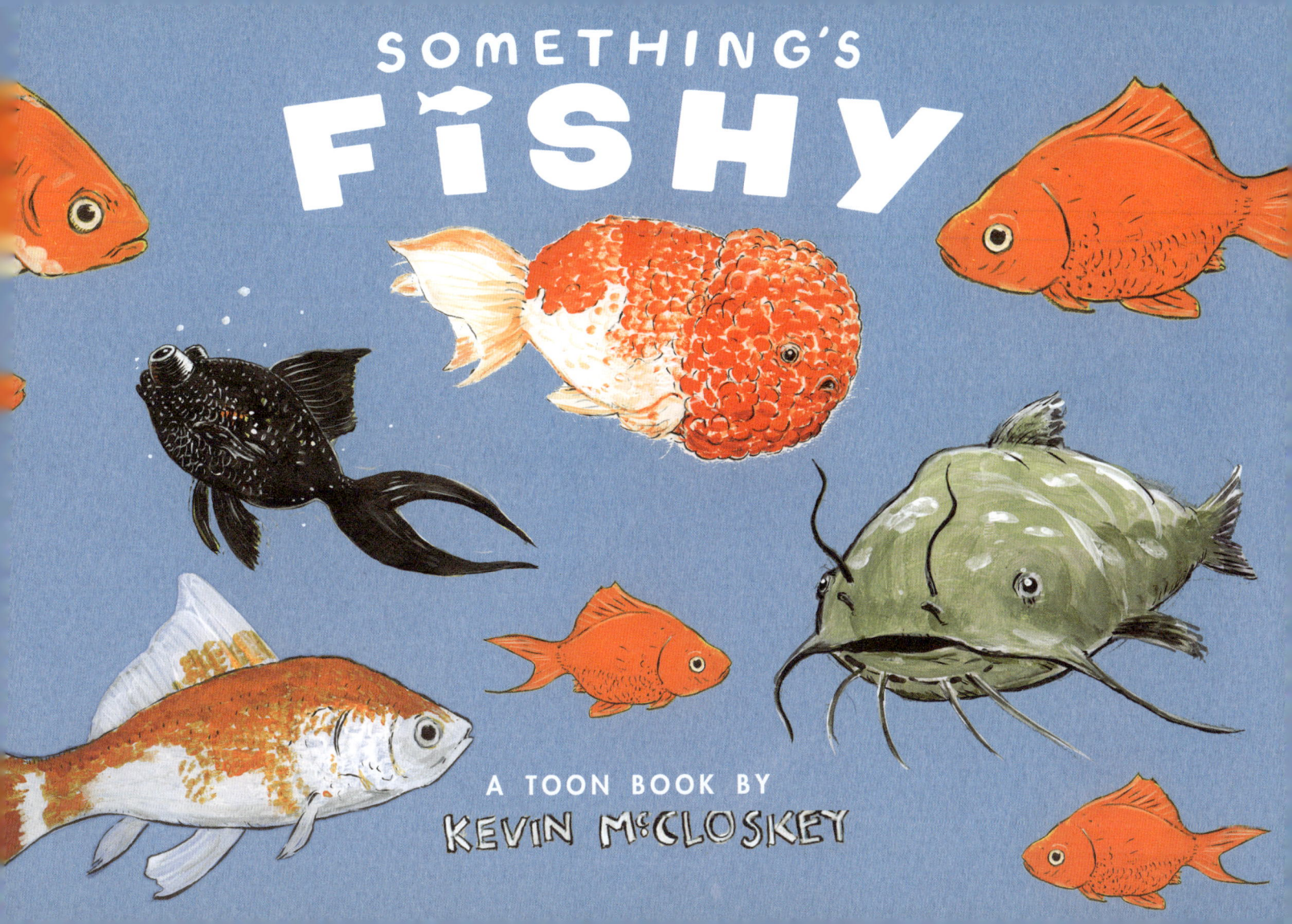

A TOON BOOK BY

## KEVIN McCLOSKEY

BIG FISH, SMALL FISH—THERE ARE SO MANY KINDS OF FISH. HERE'S ONE FOR EVERY LETTER OF THE ALPHABET.

**A**ngelfish

**B**eardfish

**C**lownfish

**D**evil Ray

2

**E**lephantnose

**F**ootballfish

**G**oatfish

**H**ammerhead
Shark

**K**issing Gourami
KISS KISS...

**L**antern Fish
THEY GLOW!
REALLY!

**I**cefish

**J**ellynose

**M**onkeyface Prickleback

4

**N**oodlefish

**P**encilfish

**R**ainbow Trout

**O**range Roughy
HE HAS A HEART
OF GOLD...

**Q**uillback Rockfish
BUT THIS GUY IS A
MEANY...

**T**iger Shark

**S**quirrelfish

**U**nicorn Fish
HE MAY BE MY FAVORITE...

**V**iperfish

**X**-ray Tetra

**Y**ellow Tang

**W**ahoo

OR MAYBE
THIS GUY IS!

**Z**ebra Fish

FISH HAVE GILLS TO BREATHE, NOT LUNGS LIKE US.

Air
LUNGS
LUNGS

WATER
GILLS

ALMOST ALL FISH.

LUNGFISH CAN BREATHE WITH THEIR GILLS OR BY GULPING AIR.

MUDSKIPPERS GO IN AND OUT
OF THE WATER AND WALK ON THEIR FINS.

MOST FISH LIVE ONLY IN WATER,
BUT SOME FISH CAN FLY...

...AND THE CHOCOLATE STARFISH.

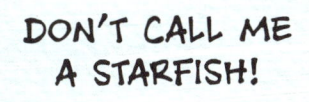 DON'T CALL ME A STARFISH!

 NO!

I'M A CHOCOLATE **SEA STAR**!

MANY PEOPLE WANT THE FISH THEY SEE IN CARTOON MOVIES.

THESE ARE RARE AND HARD TO KEEP ALIVE IN A HOME TANK.

GOLDFISH GET THEIR COLOR FROM THE SUN.

WITHOUT THE SUN, THEY'D BE **BLACK** FISH.

WHEN GOLDFISH CAME TO EUROPE, THERE WERE VERY FEW. THEY WERE GIVEN AS **VERY** SPECIAL GIFTS.

NICE!

PEOPLE WOULD INVITE FRIENDS OVER TO WATCH THEM.

NICE!

27

## A WELL-CARED-FOR GOLDFISH...

## CAN LIVE TWENTY-FIVE YEARS!

# ABOUT THE AUTHOR

Kevin McCloskey is the author of the critically acclaimed TOON Books Giggle and Learn series, which also includes *The Real Poop on Pigeons!*, *We Dig Worms!*, *Snails Are Just My Speed!*, and *Ants Don't Wear Pants!*. He used to teach illustration at Kutztown University, in Pennsylvania. Kevin says he discovered many things about goldfish thanks to his son, Daniel. "When he was a teenager, Daniel dug a small pond about the size of a bathtub. It was soon covered with water lillies," Kevin remembers. "Every winter the pond freezes over, but when spring comes, the fish are still alive. You see them when the ice becomes clear, all lined up next to the pump. I find that amazing. Neighborhood kids have brought us the fish they won at fairs. It's been almost twenty years and we now have about seventeen fish." Kevin adds, "I should point out that the various fish in this book would not all live in the same places. Some are deep-sea fish, and some are freshwater fish. I'm no scientist, but I love to learn by observing little creatures, especially those who live in my own backyard."

# HOW TO READ COMICS WITH KIDS

Kids love comics! They are naturally drawn to the details in the pictures, which make them want to read the words. Comics beg for repeated readings and let both emerging and reluctant readers enjoy complex stories with a rich vocabulary. But since comics have their own grammar, here are a few tips for reading them with kids:

**GUIDE YOUNG READERS:** Use your finger to show your place in the text, but keep it at the bottom of the character speaking so it doesn't hide the very important facial expressions.

**HAM IT UP!** Think of the comic book story as a play, and don't hesitate to read with expression and intonation. Assign parts or get kids to supply the sound effects, a great way to reinforce phonics skills.

**LET THEM GUESS.** Comics provide lots of context for the words, so emerging readers can make informed guesses. Like jigsaw puzzles, comics ask readers to make connections, so check children's understanding by asking "What's this character thinking?" (but don't be surprised if a kid finds some of the comics' subtle details faster than you).

**TALK ABOUT THE PICTURES.** Point out how the artist paces the story with pauses (silent panels) or speeded-up action (a burst of short panels). Discuss how the size and shape of the panels convey meaning.

**ABOVE ALL, ENJOY!** There is of course never one right way to read, so go for the shared pleasure. Once children make the story happen in their imagination, they have discovered the thrill of reading, and you won't be able to stop them. At that point, just go get them more books, and more comics.

## www.TOON-BOOKS.com

SEE OUR FREE ONLINE CARTOON MAKERS, LESSON PLANS, AND MUCH MORE